Shoes and Slippers

Shoes and Slippers

by Althea Mackenzie

Special Photography by Richard Blakey

THE NATIONAL TRUST

Introduction

The Wade Collection is not only one of the major collections of costume owned by the National Trust, but also represents a private collection of world-class quality. Its creator, Charles Paget Wade, was born in 1883. His father was part-owner of a family sugar plantation in St Kitts so that he was brought up in comfortable circumstances, although his childhood with his grandmother in Great Yarmouth in Norfolk was spartan. An instinct for collecting was acquired early, along with a strong sense of place and heritage.

However, the world around him was rapidly changing, compounded by the social, political and economic impact of the First World War. For Wade, this meant that much of what he had relied on as a valuable reference was being destroyed by a society that looked away from the past, and forward to a notion of progress based on material wealth and mass production. Traditional modes and mores were seen as unsustainable and undesirable.

Wade's response was to begin collecting objects that had been produced by man's hands rather than by machine. This was very much in tune with the ideals and beliefs of exponents of the Arts & Crafts Movement, such as the architects M.H.Baillie Scott and Sir Edwin Lutyens. In 1919 he bought Snowshill, a derelict but largely unspoilt Cotswold manor, and set about restoring the house and garden drawing on the fundamental principles of Arts & Crafts.

The manor house at Snowshill was the repository for his collections, which covered an astonishing range, from scientific instruments to samurai armour, from cabinets to clocks, from bicycles to kitchen bygones. Wade himself lived in the next door priest's house, to give over maximum space to the objects. In 1948 he decided to hand over his house, gardens and collections to the National Trust. James Lees-Milne, who was responsible for negotiating the transfer of houses to the care of the Trust, found Wade the most eccentric of all the owners he had to deal with – no mean feat in a contest replete with eccentric contenders.

In his diary, Lees-Milne drew a vivid pen portrait of Wade: 'Wearing square-cut, shoulder-length, Roundhead hair and dressed in trunk and hose, this magpie collector would, while showing visitors over the house, suddenly disappear behind a tapestry panel to emerge through a secret door on a different level.'

Wade was, in fact, wearing some examples from his magnificent costume collection. This consists of over 2,200 items, the majority dating from the 18th and 19th centuries, many unique and most of astounding quality. Geographically the collection incorporates material from diverse cultures; for example, from Africa, Russia and the Middle East. Historically it provides a comprehensive record of changing fashions before the impact of uniformity brought about the effects of industrial revolution and mass production. The range is vast: 18th- and 19th-century dresses (many unaltered), complete men's suits from the 18th century, beautifully embroidered 18th- and 19th-century men's waistcoats, military uniforms, servants' clothes, ecclesiastical costume, accessories such as hats and shoes. The collection is unusual in that Wade valued the utilitarian and mundane as well as the rare and precious.

Originally Wade kept the costume collection in cupboards, drawers and on display in Occidens, a room so named to evoke associations of the west and the setting sun. The clothes also provided an authentic wardrobe for some of the amateur dramatics that were performed at Snowshill, with friends such as John Betjeman, J.B.Priestley, Lutyens and Virginia Woolf. He intended that a special gallery should be built, but the plan was abandoned with the outbreak of the Second World War. On behalf of the National Trust, the collection was looked after and catalogued by the costume historian Nancy Bradfield, and subsequently by the Trust's own conservators at their studio at Blickling Hall in Norfolk.

Now, while all the other collections remain at Snowshill, the costumes and accessories are housed at Berrington Hall in Herefordshire. Because of the constraints of space, it is primarily a reserve collection available for viewing by appointment. The vulnerability innate in costume restricts display opportunities, although portions of the collection are regularly on display at Snowshill and at Berrington. However, access is vital, and this volume, the second of a series illustrated with specially commissioned photographs, is one way of enabling readers world-wide to enjoy such an important collection.

Women's shoes, as with other items of apparel, follow the vagaries of fashion. What is essentially a protective covering for the foot has become a means of conveying not just status, class and persona but hopes, dreams and fantasies. Even before the 20th century when it became acceptable for the female leg to be more exposed, the shoe held a mystery hinting at greater delights above. Shoes were worn with stockings which were frequently of bright colours, often decorated with elaborate clocks (the area covering the ankle, see p.44) to draw attention to the feet.

Shoemaking, or cordwaining, the word derived from Cordova, the Spanish town where leather was made, was often described as the 'gentle art'. By the 12th century, guilds had been established, in particular in the cities of London, Oxford and Northampton. The Snowshill collection of shoes covers the years from the early 18th to the late 19th centuries, a period of incredible change in economic and social conditions in Britain. As with so many of the local 18th-century crafts that fed local demand, shoemaking gradually became a sophisticated trade responding to the stimulus and demand of an increasingly wealthy and numerous middle class. The first textbook on shoemaking was de Garsault's *L'Art du Cordonnier* published in 1767. In 1813 John Rees published *Art and Mystery of a Cordwainer*.

The process of manufacture was slow to change. In the 16th century riveting was replaced by welting, the technique whereby the welt, insole and upper were sewn together before being attached to the sole. At the same time, the upper arrangement of vamp and two quarters seamed at the back was adopted (see diagram on p.95).

During this period the actual procedures involved in the manufacture of shoes was largely undertaken by outworkers. But the demand for boots during first the Napoleonic and later the Crimean Wars encouraged the development of mechanisation. A machine was invented for closing the uppers, a process formerly assigned to women, and gradually the other processes traditionally done by hand were also mechanised. In 1856 the Singer sewing machine, which revolutionised the production of fashion items, was adapted for sewing leather. These changes led to a move away from the hand-crafted shoes illustrated in this book, and to the first recognisable factories being established in traditional shoe-making centres such as Northampton, Kettering and Stafford.

I would like to thank Clare Bowyer who has helped me to assemble the shoes and begin the research on them, Richard Blakey for his patience and skill in taking the photographs, Stuart Smith for his designer's artistic eye, and Margaret Willes, my publisher, assisted by Andrew Cummins for coordinating all the disparate elements, of which there have been many.

Lastly, I am grateful to the staff at Berrington Hall and Snowshill Manor for their support.

Althea Mackenzie
Curator of the Wade Costume Collection

Portrait of Henrietta Howard, Countess of Suffolk, c. 1720, now at Blickling Hall in Norfolk. The short skirt of her masque dress reveals her brocade shoes with high, red heels indicating her social status.

The early 18th-century styles represented in Wade's collection show characteristics laid down in the previous century: high heels, high fronts with cross-over latchets, buckle fastenings and straights – soles made identical with no left or right.

The dispersal of wealth as a consequence of increasing trading opportunities had a tremendous impact on society. Those with status and money were keen to display these in any material way available, in housing, art and fashion. Even shoes provided a vehicle for this. The style of this pair reflects this confidence. The red heel, for instance, had been adopted from the 1660s by aristocrats as a symbol of their status. It was a fashion that lasted through to the 1770s when changes in social attitudes had a radical influence on dress style.

These shoes have uppers of pink silk with a silk top-binding and contrasting pink stitching. The shallow toes are blunt with up-curved points and a Louis heel. This shape, splayed at the base and waisted, originated at the court of Louis XIV. The heels are covered with red leather and have white contrasting edge-stitching. The rands and top-pieces are of white kid and the soles of brown leather decorated with a triangle of punch marks. Straps extend from the quarters to the vamp throat and are fastened with cream ribbon ties through single eyelets. The lining is of white kid to the quarters and the heel, and white linen to the vamp with a brown leather insole. The construction, whereby the shoe is made 'inside out', is known as turnshoe. The side and back seams are covered with silk ribbon with pink stitching. The shoes are decorated with a wide strip of silver braid which goes from the toe to the vamp tongue. One shoe is marked with the initial 'E' in ink.

Heel: 7.6cms/3ins
Size: 18.7cms/7³⁄₈ins

Shoe Early 18th century

Sir Rowland Winn, a portrait painted by Henry Pickering in 1746, now at Nostell Priory in Yorkshire. He is wearing buckled shoes very similar in style to the shoe shown opposite.

This shoe, with its plain, sensibly practical heel, could have been made for a man or a woman, illustrating the closeness of the fashions at this time. It is made from black satin with a blunt, oval and upturned toe. The heel is low, covered and shaped. The sole continues to the heel breast and is straight. The quarters extend to the latchet which crosses at the vamp fastening with a black painted metal buckle. The extra ribbons at the heel are a later addition. The lining is of white kid and linen.

Heel: 3.5cms/1 3/8 ins
Size: 23.5cms/9 1/4 ins

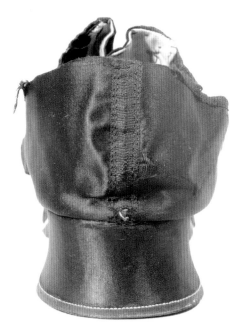

A pair of brocade shoes made in the 1720s, now in the costume collection at Killerton in Devon. Remarkably, their original protective overshoes have also survived.

Before the 17th century, clogs were synonymous with pattens and were worn by both sexes as protection from mud and dirt. During the 1600s pattens with leather soles on attached iron rings were introduced and became universal country wear eventually to be associated with the lower working classes. The favourite wood for clogs was alder, twenty-five to thirty years old. Alder was straight-grained, water-resistant and not prone to splitting. The clog-maker would usually be itinerant within a region, roughing out clog blocks for drying out before final shaping.

Ladies of higher status wore special clogs or clog overshoes, often designed to match a particular pair of shoes. They generally followed the uniform style with a built-up instep, a long flat sole that extended slightly beyond the shoe end and latchets that tied over the front of the shoe. It was only when shoes became more robust and made of more durable materials that such protection was redundant.

The clog, above right, dating from the 1720s, has a red leather and velvet upper lined with wool and decorated with a green binding of wool ribbon with white contrasting stitching on the instep and the sock edge. The sole is of black leather. The toe is needlepoint (see p.12)

and the heel is stacked with a top-piece of leather. The sole is straight and shows much wear.

Heel: none
Size: 22.3cms/8¾ ins

The pair of sewn clogs, below right, also dating from the 1720s, has red leather straps lined with white leather, wedge heels and brown leather soles. The toes are pointed. The soles are straights that continue to the heel slap. The side straps fasten over the front or vamp of the shoe with a single lace (now both missing).

Heel: none
Size: 22.3cms/8¾ ins

Brocade Shoes 1720s

Detail of an open robe of woven silk, made for the Strickland family at Sizergh Castle in Cumbria. The matching shoes have also survived.

Eighteenth-century shoes were generally made from fabric until the 1770s when kid and leather were increasingly used. Although the fabric could be chosen to accompany a particular dress, it was not until the end of the century that the concept of matching, co-ordinated accessories became the norm. As with so many aspects of dress during the period, the emphasis was on the display of wealth through costliness and excess of the fabrics and trimmings. French brocades enjoyed the reputation for being the most exotic and desirable during the first years of the century, but it was not long before English

fabrics were competing in quality and design. The silk brocade with its bold floral pattern of the dress shown left was woven in Spitalfields in East London in the early 1740s.

The shoes are made of cream silk brocade with a turquoise and pink floral design on the uppers, and heel covers with cream silk binding. They have white kid rands and brown suede soles. The toes are pointed and upcurved with the upper overhanging the sole. This style is known as needlepoint, which should not be confused with embroidery. The soles are straights and continue to the heel breast. The dog-leg side seams continue

to latchets which cross the front of the shoe. There is a yellow ochre linen lining with a leather insole. The shoes are of turnshoe construction.

Heel: 5.1cms/2 ins
Size: 21cms/8¼ ins

Brocade Shoes 1735

Shoes made from a rich silk brocade of green, pink, brown, and cream, attributed by the costume historian Natalie Rothstein to English manu-facture, 1735-6. The toes have a blunt, slightly domed point. The soles are straights of brown leather which continue to the heel breast. The heels are covered with the same brocade, and shaped with top-pieces of leather. The latchets cross over the vamp to reveal a square tongue. The quarters and vamp are lined with yellow linen and there is a brown leather insole.

They are of turnshoe construction with a white kid rand. Latchets, vamp tongue and top seams are bound with binding of green linen and silk. 'Br 5 23' is written on the vamp of both shoes in ink.

Heel: 6cms/2ins
Size: 20cms/7ins

Heels 18th-century

This series of photographs shows how heels evolved during the 18th century, moving towards a finer, more delicate profile. The final development in the early 19th century was the flat slipper, the fashionable style for several decades.

Top row, left to right:
At the beginning of the century, heels were high, this example measures 7.6cms/3ins. It is red, indicating a claim to aristocratic status, and shows the splayed back and waist of the Louis shape (see pp.6 and 7).

A heel measuring 5.1cms/2ins from the 1720s, covered in cream silk brocade (see pp. 12 and 13).

A Louis heel from the 1740s, in mustard yellow satin. It is very high, measuring 8.9cms/3½ins (see pp.22 and 23).

Bottom row, left to right:
A heel from c.1770, covered in cream satin. It still has a Louis shape, measuring 5.4cms/ 2⅛ins (see pp. 36 and 37).

A heel from the 1780s in black leather. It has the fashionable Italian or peg shape. The height is much lower than earlier in the century, 2.8cms/1⅛in (see pp. 44 and 45).

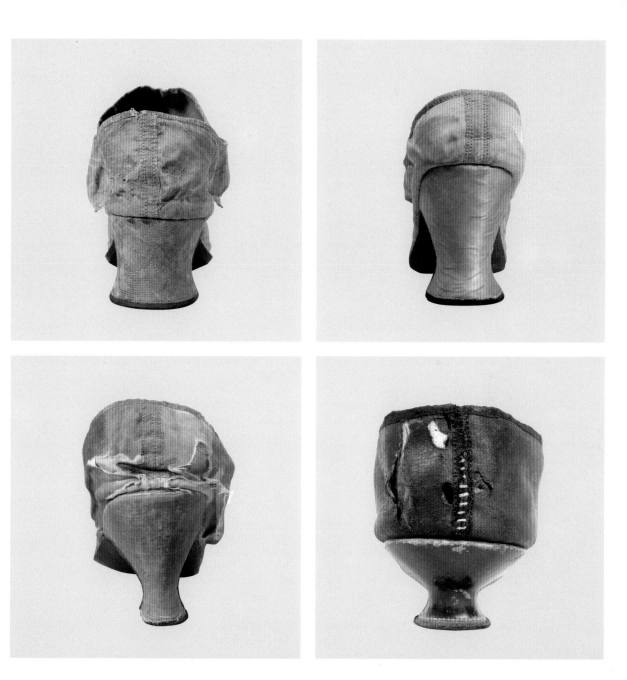

Shoes 1740s

As the proportions of shoes became lighter, a more pointed and upturned toe developed as a characteristic feature. In the 1740s, buckle fastenings took over from the ties as seen on p. 7. The buckle, adopted for both male and female dress, provided yet another opportunity to exhibit status and wealth (see pp. 34 and 35).

The pair of shoes, above left and right, would have been enhanced by a buckle. The uppers and heel covers are of raspberry silk with matching top seam binding. The soles are straights of brown leather. The toes are typically needlepoint and upturned. The Louis shaped heels have a top-piece of leather. The shoes have back straps and butted straight seams squared off to extend to latchets. They are lined with white leather kid, white linen and they have a brown leather sock. The construction is turnshoe, and they have a white leather rand.

Heel: 5.7cms/2¼ ins
Size: 22.5cms/8⅞ins

The single shoe, below right, is made from a bunting yellow silk brocade dated by Natalie Rothstein to 1740-3. The upper is bound with bunting yellow silk and the lining is of cream linen. The brown leather sole is decorated with punch holes and continues to the top piece of the Louis shaped heel. The toe has a blunt and upturned point. It has a closed back and dog-legged closed side seam. The latchets would have buckled over the vamp to reveal a squared tongue. It is a turnshoe construction. There is a label 'J R' written in ink on the reverse of the tongue and a further indecipherable figure.

Heel: 5.7cms/2¼ ins
Size: 26.7cms/10½ ins

Shoes 1740

Detail from a group portrait of the Duncombe family by Andrea Soldi painted in 1741 and now at Duncombe Park in Yorkshire. The young lady is raising her skirt to show her rich petticoat and a pink shoe with up turned toe and braid decoration.

These shoes are a good example of the development towards a less rigid, more flowing design in footwear. Buckles have replaced ties, the heel is lower and lighter, the design is more flamboyant with silver braid decoration.

This pair has cream damask uppers and shaped heels with brown leather soles. The toes are blunt and slightly domed. The soles are straights with punch holes at the instep and toe. The latchets, damaged in the buckle area, cross over and reveal squared-off tongues. The lining is of cream linen with a brown leather insole. There is white stitching at the seam edges and a white kid rand. The shoes are decorated with a silver metal brocade band centrally from toe to vamp tongue. The top seam has a ribbon binding that extends to the latchets.

Silver, woven, embroidered or applied, was frequently used in decoration. Silver-gilt braid on shoes was always referred to as lace. In a letter written by the Purefoy family in 1744, there is reference to the purchase of 'enough of fashionable silver lace to lace four pairs of shoes for my mother, and a yard of narrow silver lace to go up the seam behind the shoes'.

Heel: 6.4cms / 2½ ins
Size: 18.5cms / 7½ ins

Although relatively plain, the next two shoes rely on the richness of their fabric and the contrasting white stitching for their impact.

The upper and heel of the shoe above are of exquisite emerald green damask which has been dated by Natalie Rothstein to 1742-4 and of probable English manufacture. The brown leather sole is straight, has punch marks at the instep, toe and heel and continues to the heel breast. The shaped heel is enhanced by white stitching to the edges. The toe is needlepoint, upturned with a toe stiffener. The upper has a squared tongue and the sides extend to the latchets which cross over the vamp. The quarters and vamp are lined with white leather with a canvas tongue and a brown leather sock. It is of a turnshoe construction. The white leather rand provides a striking contrast to the emerald green of the upper.

Heel: 7.6cms/3 ins
Size: 22.8 cms/8 ins

The shoe, right, is made of mustard yellow satin with a brown leather straight sole with a round tread. This continues to the heel breast and the Louis shaped heel. The toe is blunt and slightly domed. The shoe has a back strap and angled side butted seams. The quarters extend to latchets over the vamp and reveal a square tongue. It is lined with white kid from the quarters to the latchets and the vamp is lined with white linen with a facing of 2.5cms/1in silk. It is of a turnshoe construction with decorative white stitching at the heel edge.

Heel: 8.9cms/3½ ins
Size: 16.8cms/6⅝ ins

Brocade shoes 1740s

A portrait of Sir John and Elizabeth, Lady Pole, painted by Thomas Hudson in 1755 and now at Antony House in Cornwall. Lady Pole is daringly showing her ankle and fashionably high-heeled shoe of white satin with a silver buckle.

Eighteenth-century diaries and wills testify to the innate value of silks that were specified as gifts with a realisable monetary value. As a result, there was a thriving second-hand industry. Items were passed to servants or reused for accessories, which is presumably what happened with the brocade used for these shoes that has been dated by Natalie Rothstein to c.1725 and re-used fifteen to twenty-five years later.

The uppers are made from a cream, green, pink, blue, maroon and grey brocade with a green top seam binding. The shaped heels are covered with white damask. The brown leather soles are straight and continue to the heel breast. The toes are blunt and slightly domed. The sides extend to latchets to cross over the tongues which are pointed rather than the more usual square. The shoes are lined with cream linen on the quarters and vamp and have brown leather insoles. They are of a turnshoe construction.

Heel: 6cms/2³⁄₈ ins
Size: 24.1cms/9¹⁄₂ ins

Mules 1750s

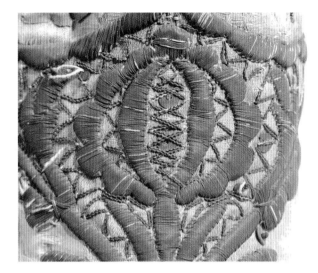

Mules were a French fashion, worn indoors for both formal and informal occasions. Although impractical, they were very elegant. The term mule was originally used in the 16th century but went out of fashion by the late 18th century, to be revived in the 19th century.

This pair is of pink satin with white leather-covered French or Pompadour heels and brown leather soles. The toes are pointed and overhang the sole. The soles are straights that continue to the heel breast. There are no quarters and the vamps are cut to a small point with the edges terminating at the arch. The rands are white stitched. There is a lining of white leather with a white leather sock. They are of a welted construction. Silver metal floral embroidery decorates the vamps.

Heel: 6.4cms/2½ ins
Size: 16.5cms/6½ ins

Shoe 1760s

This shoe illustrates well the precariousness of the fashions of this period. The 'Receipt for Modern Dress' of 1753 warns 'Mount on French heels when you go to a ball/'Tis the fashion to totter and show you fall.'

This shoe has a narrow French heel with a leather triangular top-piece which gives a sharp outline up the back of the heel. The upper is made from a gold/champagne coloured ribbed silk threaded through with silver. The latchets and heel cover are made of plain champagne satin and would have buckled over the pointed tongue. The sole is a straight of brown leather which continues to the heel breast. The

toe has a blunt point. There is a closed back seam and a straight closed side seam slanting forwards. The lining is of cream kid with a linen sock and linen lining to the vamp, apart from a small piece of green and white striped silk across the tongue. It is of a turnshoe construction. There is indecipherable writing on the kid quarters.

Heel: 9.2cms/3⅝ ins
Size: 25.4cms/10 ins

Leather shoes 1770s

The leather shoes shown with a cotton polonaise of the 1770s, and a modern yellow petticoat.

Until the 1770s, leather had been associated with working-class footwear. But the obvious advantages of leather with its greater potential for support and protection led to its increasing use for luxury footwear. These beautifully-made examples display all the features of shoes for an upper-class lady and would have been fastened with delicate and elaborate silver buckles.

The red leather forms the uppers and the heel covers of these shoes. They have brown leather straight soles that continue to the heel breast. The toes are pointed, blunt and domed. The covered Louis heels have top-pieces of leather. The vamps of the upper continue to a pointed tongue and the quarters extend to latchets which cross at the vamp. There is a butted back seam. This and the top edge of the quarters and vamp tongues are covered with ribbon. There is a white linen sock lining with a white kid stiffener from vamp to heel oversewn with leather. There is no lining to the quarters. The shoes are of a turnshoe construction.

This style often accompanied the polonaise, a short open gown worn above the ankle, with a draped overskirt that was pulled up by drawstrings. The polonaise allowed a greater show of both ankle and footwear, so that accessories such as sashes might be matched with the shoes.

Heel: 5.5cms/2¼ ins
Size: 22.2cms/8¾ ins

Shoes 1760s–'80s

The pair, above right, dates from between 1766 and 1775. Delicate in style, the shoes have uppers and heel covers of cream fancy-ribbed silk. The toes have blunted and domed points that curve up slightly. The heels are of a wedge shape, possibly Italian, with a top-piece of leather. The brown suede soles are straights and extend to the heel breast. There are covered, butted back seams and straight closed side seams that extend to the latchets which cross and fasten over pointed tongues. The lining is of white linen.

Heel: 7cms/2¾ ins
Size: 25cms/9⅞ ins

The pair, below right, from the 1780s, reflect the development towards lower heels placed further underneath the shoe.

The shoes are made from black woven wool with covered heels and brown leather soles. The toes are blunt and the heels are Italian shape with top-pieces of leather. The soles are shaped, continuing to the heel breast with polished sides at the waist of each sole. The latchets extend from the quarters to cross over pointed tongues. There are back seams and side seams that slant forward. The lining is of white linen with a white linen sock. Inside the vamp is written 'Miss Molly'.

Heel: 3.8cms/1½ ins
Size: 26.7cms/10½ ins

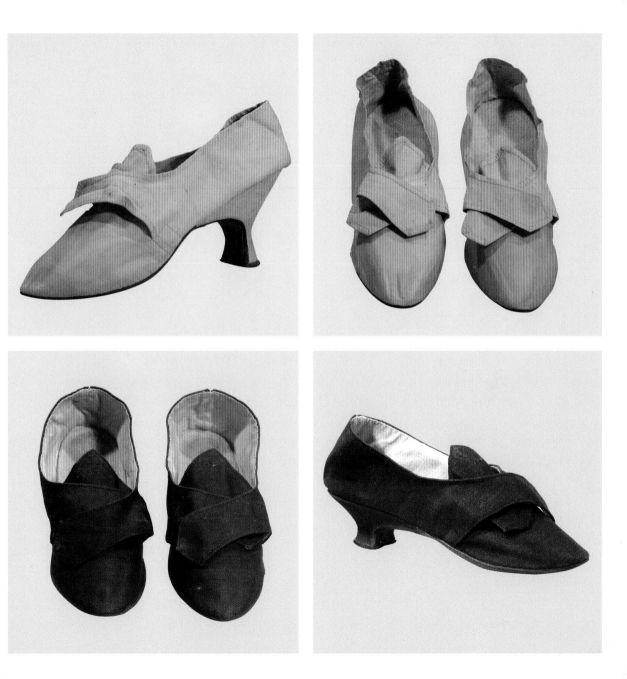

Buckles

Buckles replaced ties as the fastenings for shoes in the 1740s. They were made from a variety of materials such as steel, silver, Sheffield plate, gilded brass, were generally rectangular, square or oval, and could be decorated with precious or semi-precious jewels according to wealth, status or aspiration. Josiah Wedgwood even invented a white earthenware buckle in 1779 and marketed it as pearlware. Most of the silver buckles were cast and chased, and many were set with glass paste. So popular was the use of glass paste that an excise was levied on it in 1777.

The great buckle - making centres in the 18th century –

Wolverhampton, Birmingham and Bilston – were all based in the English Midlands. Matthew Boulton, the great entrepreneur from Birmingham, told a committee of the House of Commons in 1775 of 8,000 people being employed in the area with an annual return of £300,000. By the end of the century, however, the wearing of buckles went into decline with the development of slippers. This caused great hardship to the buckle-makers and chape-makers (the makers of the iron working parts of the buckle), who petitioned the Prince of Wales to no great avail.

This pair of silver buckles dates from the 1770s. They are

for ladies' shoes, and tended to be smaller and more restrained than men's buckles because they were not such an obvious feature of dress.

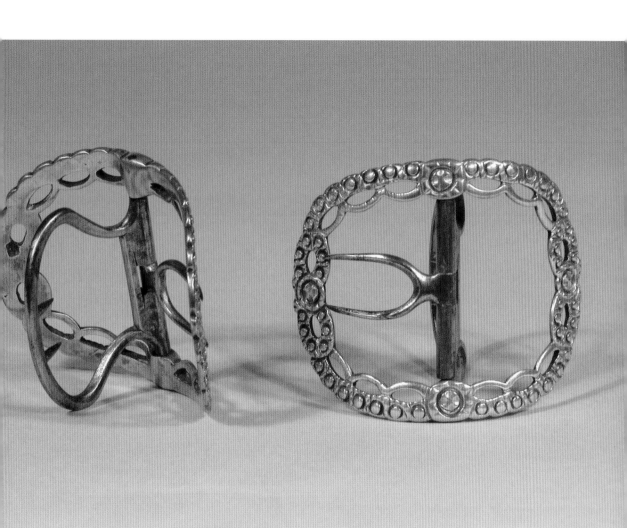

Shoe *c.* 1770

This single shoe has a cream upper with green latchets and heel cover. The vamp is of satin and the latchet and binding of taffeta. The toe is pointed and domed. The Louis heel has a top-piece of leather. The brown leather sole is shaped, slightly rounded and continues to the heel breast. The back quarters have a back seam and back strap and the side quarters extend to the latchets which cross over a pointed tongue. The lining is white linen with a leather insole. The shoe is of a turnshoe construction. There is metal floral embroidery and sequins decorating the vamp.

Heel: 5.4cms / 2⅛ ins
Size: 22.2cms / 8¾ ins

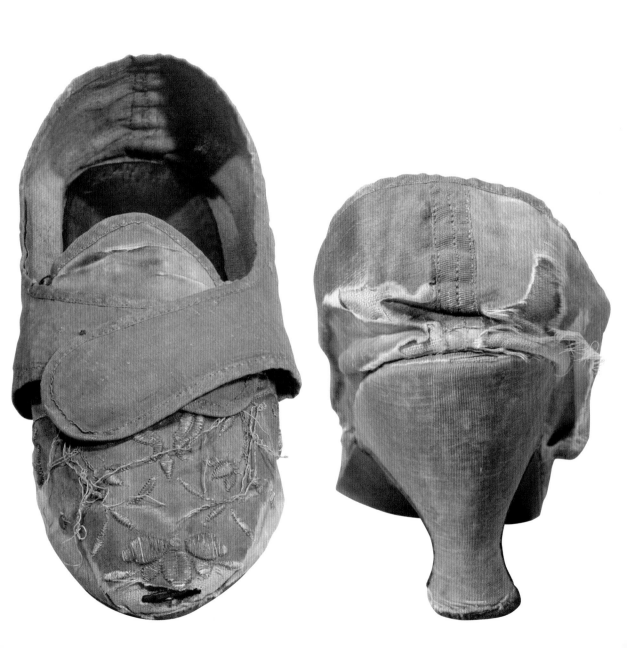

Shoe 1770-86

Portrait of an unknown lady by A.W. Devis from the late 1780s, now at Wimpole Hall in Cambridgeshire. She is wearing peg-heeled shoes with a swirling dress of delicate lace.

One of a pair of very feminine shoes made from cream ribbed silk with shell pink satin latchets and heel cover. The toe is pointed, blunt and upcurved. The heel is thin and wedged with a top-piece of leather. The brown suede sole is straight with three punch marks and a polished strip from the waist to the top-piece.

It has a butted back seam, forward slanting side seams and latchets that cross over a pointed tongue. It is lined throughout in cream linen. The shoe is of turnshoe construction. The latchets, tongue, quarters and back seam are all decorated with pink ribbon binding.

Heel: 6cms/2³⁄₈ ins
Size: 24cms/9¹⁄₂ ins

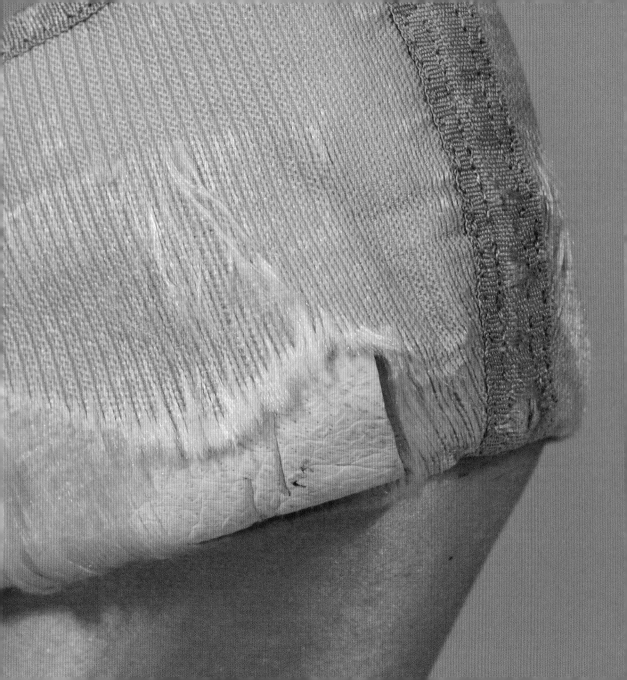

Shoes 1780s

This pair of shoes would have
been worn without buckles and
provide a good example of the
move towards the peg heel and
flat slipper. They are made from
black leather and fasten with
a fine piece of cord threaded
through the top binding,
fastening under the tongue.
The toes are blunt. The brown
leather soles are straights that
continue to the top-piece. There
are closed back and side seams
and the vamps have pointed
tongues. They are lined with
cream linen and have brown
leather socks. They are of
turnshoe construction.

Heel: 4.5cms/1¾ ins
Size: 28cms/11 ins

Shoes 1775-85

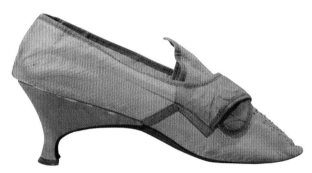

This is a finely shaped pair of shoes made from a beige and pink silk and 'spor weave' silk. The toes are blunt, pointed and slightly domed. The heels are shaped, possibly Italian, with top-pieces of leather. The brown leather soles are straight and have small punch holes at the toe and waist and polished leather strips at heel sides from the waist to the top-piece. The uppers have back straps and strips of leather covering the back seams. There are shaped side seams extending to the latchets which cross over the vamp over a pointed tongue. The linings are of white kid and linen. The top seam binding and latchets are of pink silk, and ribbon has been threaded into the vamp silk to give the effect of French knot embroidery. They are of a turnshoe construction.

Heel: 6cms/ 2⅜ ins
Size: 20cms/ 7⅞ ins

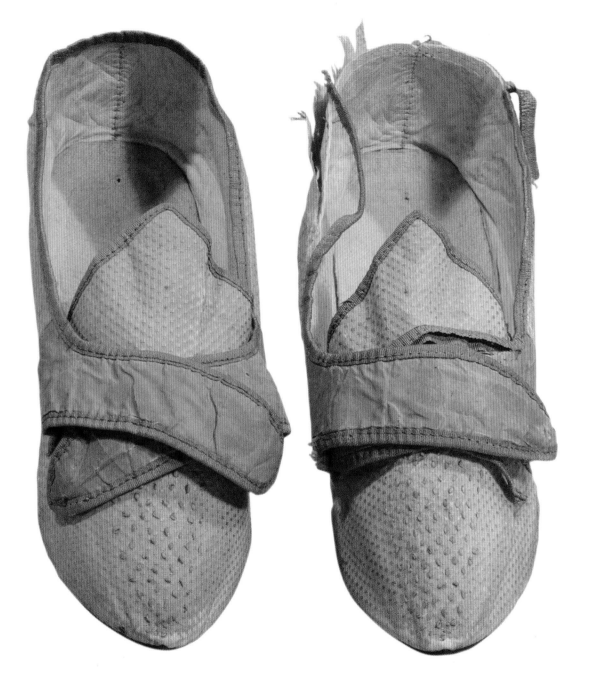

Peg-heeled Shoes 1780s

Stockings from the costume collection at Killerton, dating from the 17th, 18th and 19th centuries. They are all decorated with clocks.

Low-heeled shoes became popular at this time, often made in pale colours to match the fashionably light muslin dresses or coloured stitching on stockings. The delicate peg heels were celebrated in verse in the *Gentleman's Magazine* in 1776: 'Heels to bear the precious charge,/More diminutive than large,/Slight and brittle, apt to break,/Of the true Italian make.'

The single shoe, above right, has a black glazed wool upper with a black leather heel cover. The toe is needlepoint and slightly domed. The heel is Italian shaped with a top-piece of leather. The straight brown leather sole is shaped with two scoring lines down the waist of the sole. The sole continues to the heel breast as on a Louis heel. There is a back strap and a butted, covered side seam. The quarters are lined with white leather and the vamp and sock with white linen. There is a brown leather three-quarter insole and a heel grip. The shoe is decorated with white contrasting stitching on the heel edge and the waist of sole edges. The waist of the sole is also polished with punch marks at toe and waist.

Heel: 2.8cms/1$\frac{1}{8}$ ins
Size: 25cms/9$\frac{7}{8}$ ins

The shoe, below right, is made from green and white leather uppers with a white leather-covered, Italian-shaped heel. The toe is pointed and slightly domed. The brown leather sole is a straight which continues to the heel breast. There is a pointed tongue. The lining of the quarters, vamp and sock are of white linen and the insole is of brown leather. It is a turnshoe construction. It is decorated with a white strap ribbon over the side and back seams with a pleated rosette of white silk on the vamp throat. There are punchmarks on the sole at the toe and waist and inside it has a label (see p. 52).

Heel: 4.5cms/1$\frac{3}{4}$ ins
Size: 23.2cms/9$\frac{1}{4}$ ins

Exotic Slippers 1780s

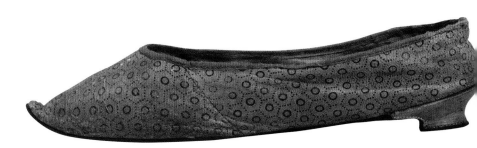

During the 18th century, fashion was influenced by the increasing trade with and travel to countries such as India and China. These slippers are designed for summer wear: the winter equivalent was known as the Kampskatcha slipper. But the Far East was not the only source of inspiration. The Middle East too provided a rich resource, particularly after Napoleon's campaigns in Egypt. Ancient Egyptian became the fashionable style for everything from furniture and clocks to jewellery and footwear. By the Victorian period, eclecticism was the name of the game.

In the 1760s the term slipper became interchangeable with shoe. Shoes described as slippers tended to have small, low peg heels. These slippers have uppers of kid with a yellow vamp and pink quarters. They have been printed with a black honeycomb design. The heels are wedged with a plain pink kid covering. The toes are needlepoint, domed and up-curved. The brown leather soles are straight scored with two parallel marks from the heel breast which widen out towards the edges of the soles and meet the side seams of the uppers. The soles continue to the heel breast. The back seams are butted and the side seams forward slanting. The lining is of cream linen with kid heel stiffeners. The shoes are further decorated with a lemon wool edge binding. They are of turnshoe construction.

Heel: 1.9cms/¾ in
Size: 30.5cms/12 ins

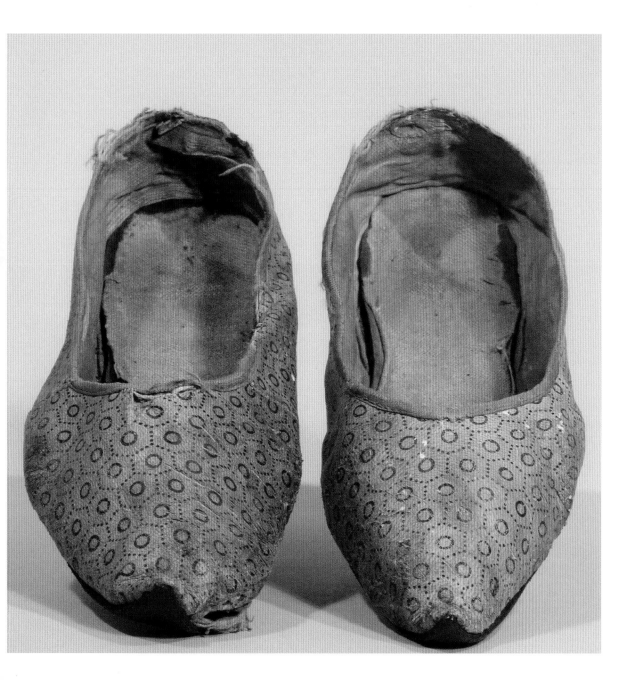

Slipper 1810

The French Revolution brought about a period of profound social change. Moreover, England was for the next twenty years involved almost continuously in Continental wars. As a result there developed a nostalgia for Greek and Roman styles and the purity and simplicity these implied. The slipper became the footwear associated with delicate muslin dresses and the refinement of manners, modes and mores. This was also a time of great revival in dance and the stage. The toes of slippers remained pointed until around 1807 when they began to be more squared off or rounded.

For the first two decades of the 19th century it was common for women to make their own slippers. In a letter of 9 September 1814, Jane Austen wrote to her niece Anna, 'your Grandmama desires me to say that she will have finished your Shoes tomorrow & thinks they will look very well'.

This example of a single slipper is characteristic of the style in fashion for several decades. It is made from green silk with ribbon binding. The toe is square and domed. The upper has no back seam but lapped side seams. The shoes would have fastened with laces from the side through a pair of tabs. The ribbon is now missing. There is white leather kid lining to the quarters and sock and white linen lining to the vamp. It is a turnshoe construction. Inside this remaining slipper 'droit' is written on the insole to remind the wearer which of the identical slippers was for the right and which for the left.

There is a silk rosette at the vamp. Rosettes and ribbons had replaced buckles as the more common feature for shoe decoration. This caused the buckle trade in Birmingham to collapse, throwing an estimated 20,000 men and women out of work.

Heel: none
Size: 22.2 cms / 8¾ ins

Slippers 1810-30

Fashion plate from Lady's Magazine for November 1817 when the whole nation was in mourning for the death in childbirth of Princess Charlotte. The model is wearing cross-laced slippers.

This pair of slippers is a fine example of the fashionable style of the early 19th century. They are made from dark rose pink silk. The toes are square and slightly domed, a typical feature from 1815 onwards. The brown leather soles are shaped with no heel, the sides having polished edges. The uppers have covered back seams and covered side seams with side silk ties of cream silk, possibly a later addition.

The Roman style of ties had its problems. According to 'The Hermit of London' writing in 1819, the cross-lacings were 'so tight that they crippled her, from which ribbons crossed her ankle and cut it at angles backwards and forwards'.

The quarters, vamps and insoles are lined with white linen and there is a heel stiffener and a brown leather heel grip. They are of turnshoe construction. The top, back and side seams are bound with dark pink cotton with contrasting white stitching.

Each slipper is marked on the inside in ink, left/right. In the left shoe a yellow label reads 'sold by T S Buttifant, London Lane, Norwich'.

Heel: none
Size: 23.5 cms/9¼ ins

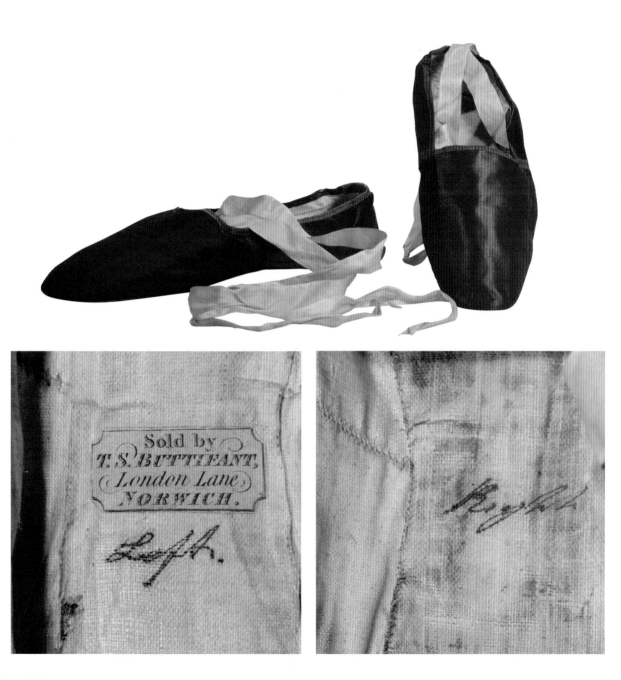

Retailing Shoes

The detail of a painting, by an unknown artist, dates from c.1830, and very unusually shows the interior of a shoe shop. The slippers are arranged with their heels facing outwards, and their ribbon ties dangling. The seated lady is being offered various pairs of slippers, plus an exotic mule in golden satin with an oriental turned-up toe. In the background is a young man also trying on shoes, with a pile of boot-shapers next to him on the floor.

In the 18th century, for the ready-made market, shoemakers sold their products through their own shops or through haberdashers. Warehouses were very much a feature of city retailing – these could either concentrate on products from a particular country, such as Italy, or on a particular item drawn from many countries, such as hats, shawls and shoes. Shopkeepers and warehousemen marketed their wares through trade cards and advertisements in local newspapers. It was also at this period that shoemakers began to place labels on the sock of the shoe.

Shoe labels:
The earliest example in Wade's collection dates from the 1780s, and reads 'Barry, Ladies Shoe Maker from Mr Dodds, Jermyn Street, St James, London, Glocester' (see also page 44).

A label in slippers from the 1830s describes F.Marsh at 148 Oxford Street as an importer of French boots and shoes (see also p.68). At this time French manufacturers were swamping the market with narrow satin shoes, generally black or white, and marked 'droit' and 'gauche'. The effect on the shoemakers of Northampton was serious

enough for attempts to be made to tax these imports, but to no avail. Many shoemakers continued to advertise 'French' shoes, although it was rumoured that they were being manufactured in London's East End.

A label in slippers from the late 1830s describes the maker, C. Mingay, as proprietor of a shoe warehouse at No.7 Old Hay Market in Norwich. These slippers are also marked with 'droit' and 'gauche' (see also p.70).

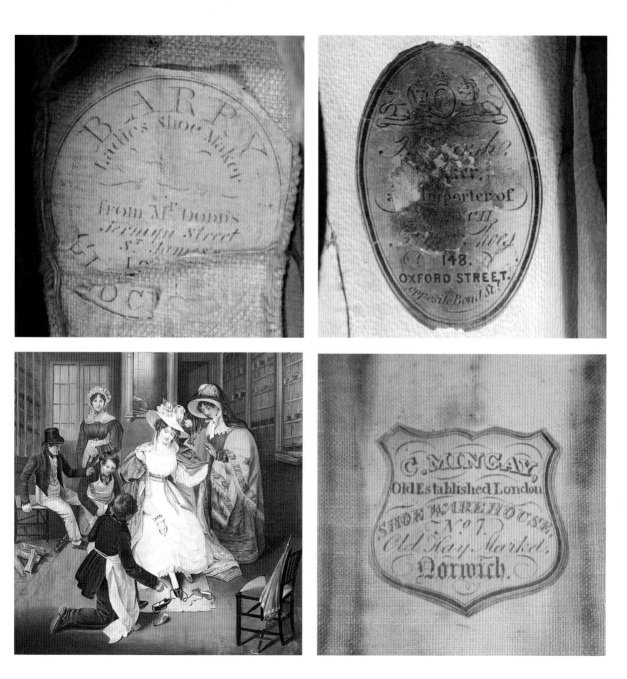

Slippers 1810

These silk slippers have been dyed blue, purple and pink to give a mother-of-pearl effect. The toes are rounded off square and domed. The brown suede soles are straights with no heel with ring stamps in a double line at the heel and sole and floral ring stamps at the sole waist and heel. There is a V-shaped cut at the vamp throat on the uppers. The vamp throats have tie fastenings with one pair of eyelets and silk ribbon ties. The quarters are lined with white kid, the sock with white silk and the vamp with white linen. They are of turnshoe construction. The top seams have a binding of cream silk that extends to the V cut.

There is a maker's label on both insoles 'MAN[L] Arcolea Vuie Plaza de Sn.Ant.[O] 22,Cadiz.'

Heel: none
Size: 23.5 cms/9¾ ins

These two pairs of cream silk slippers have been added to and altered at a later date, quite possibly by Charles Wade himself.

The pair, above right, has square toes, brown leather soles with floral stamps and wheeling along the waist and no heel. The uppers have closed side seams but no back seams. The shoes would have been fastened with ribbons through loops on the side and the back and front. The linings are of cream glazed cotton with green kid stiffener. They are of turnshoe construction. The upper edges and side seams are decorated with cream silk ribbon and later additions of decoration consisting of a piece of flower-sprigged brocade on the vamp and a ribbon with floral decoration on the uppers and vamp throats. There is also a cream rosette threaded through with silver at the vamp throats.

There is a maker's label on both consisting of the Prince of Wales feathers 'Ich Dien' 'Borsley, No 43 Wigmore Street, Cavendish Square'. 'Philips' is hand-written on the side of the vamp on the right shoe only.

Heel: none
Size: 25.4cms/10ins

The pair, below right, has square toes, shaped leather soles and no heels. There are ribbon loops at the front and back and each side of the shoes which would have contained the fastening ribbons. The shoes are decorated with a piece of brocade that is the same as that on one of the 18th-century dresses in the collection, which suggests Wade's intervention. There is also silver-threaded cream silk ribbon decoration on the quarters and vamp.

Heel: none
Size: 25.4cms/10ins

Slipper 1830s

Portrait of Mrs Robinson by William Owen, painted c.1820 and now at Petworth House in Sussex. Mrs Robinson is wearing the elegant leather slippers fashionable at this period.

This single slipper is made from black kid. The square toe is slightly domed and upcurved. The straight brown leather sole is shaped with no heel. The vamp has a scalloped edge and the upper has straight closed side seams. The quarters, heel and sock are lined with white kid and the vamp of white linen. It is of a turnshoe construction. Blue silk binding decorates the top. The vamp is further decorated with a pleated ruff scalloped in white silk which extends to the side seams and a floral motif that is embroidered in chain stitch in a floral motif over a leather cut-out with an underlay of blue silk.

According to the Pattern Book produced by the Norwich guild of shoemakers, the design is possibly by Sophia Hase dating from 1815.

Heel: none
Size: 25.4cms / 10ins

Shoes Early 19th century

This pair of pale green kid shoes has rounded and lightly domed toes with small wedge heels which became popular in the 1830s. The straight slap soles continue to the top-piece and have polished sides and punch marks at the toe and the waist. The quarters, vamps and socks are lined with white linen and there is a kid heel grip and stiffener. There are butted side seams and back straps. The vamp of each shoe is decorated with two bound cut-outs, two buckles with serrated edges and a silk tassel.

Heel: 2.2 cms/$^7/_8$ in
Size: 22.2cms/8$^3/_4$ ins

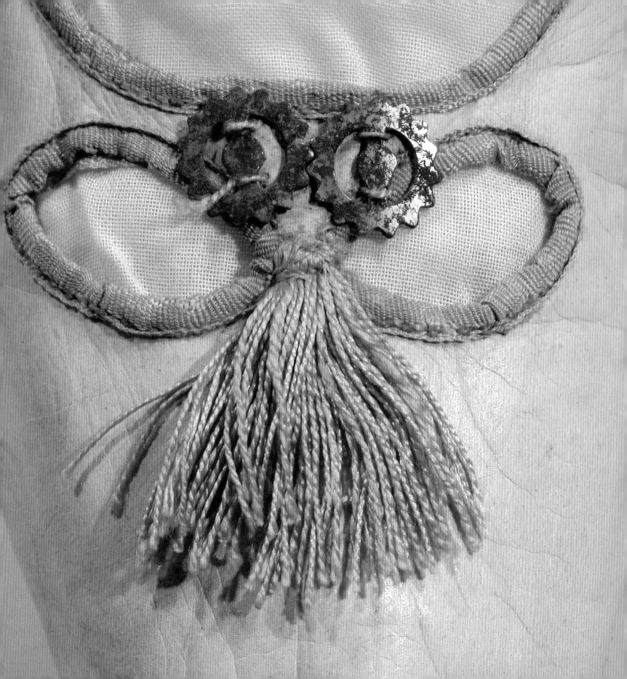

Shoe *c.* 1830

One of a fascinating pair of shoes made from plaited, woven straw over visible red silk linings. The toe is square and domed and the sole is straight, made from brown leather. The upper has a vamp with a round tongue but no back and straight side seams. The sides, vamp and sock are all lined with the red silk. It is of turnshoe construction and is decorated with two bands of plaited straw across the vamp alternating with open-work straw bands. On the tongue is a silk rosette with a straw centre. The top seams have double scalloped straw lacing and there are bands of straw at the welt which extends on each side from quarter to heel. The number '6' is written in ink on the soles of both shoes.

Heel: none
Size: 25.7 cms/10⅛ ins

Clogs 19th century

Clogs continued to be associated with the working classes, although by this time variations were emerging. One patent, taken out in 1826, refers to a wooden, hinged sole with leather toe cap and quarters with ankle strap. This pair was made following the patent, with black leather toe caps and brass quarters. The toe caps are attached with thirteen nails and the quarters with three screws. The toes are square and the heels of stacked wood with a top-piece nailed in with fourteen nails. The soles are waisted at the instep and are also stacked with thirty-two nails round the outer edge and two inside. They, too, are hinged using three narrow strips of brass over leather. The brass is held in position with screws. The uppers have leather-covered straps with four brass coils under a buckle at one side and a brass clasp at the other.

Heel: 2cms/¾ in
Size: 23.5cms/9¼ ins

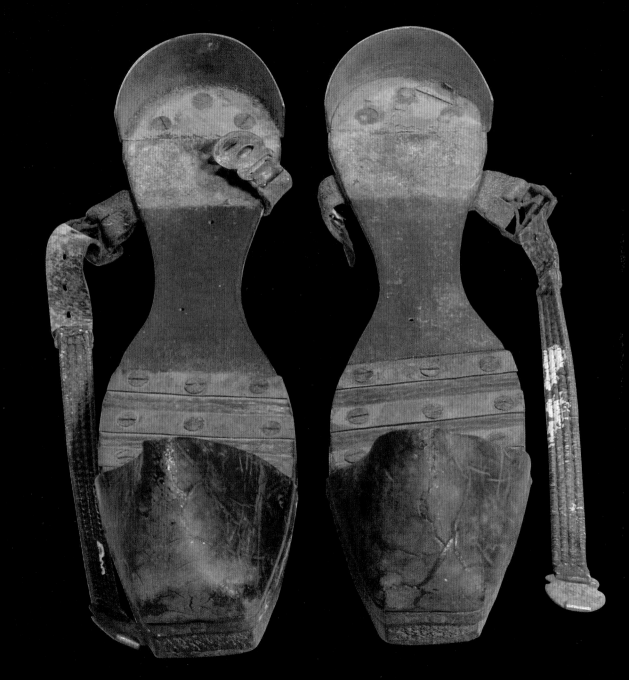

The pair above has black leather uppers, quarters, ankle straps and straps over the front of the foot, all nailed into a wooden sole. The soles are slightly shaped and worn, varying in thickness from 1.2cm/$^1/_2$ in to 1.9cm/$^3/_4$ in. They are fastened with cotton ribbon ties for ankle straps and straps across the front of the foot.

Heel: 2cms/$^3/_4$ in
Size: 26.4cms/10$^3/_8$ ins

The pair right is more traditional with black leather uppers and brown leather soles. The toes are square and the platform varies in thickness. The black leather uppers are cut from one piece of leather with solid toe caps and straps across the instep and quarters. Black cotton ribbon ties go across the front of the foot and around the ankle, and all edges of the uppers are bound in black cotton ribbon.

Heel: 2cms/$^3/_4$in
Size: 25.4cms/10ins

Slippers 1830s

French fashion plate of the 1830s showing how delicate slippers were worn with fuller skirts, gigot sleeves and huge, ornate bonnets.

These two pairs are typical of the black satin slippers that were so popular in the early Victorian period. The rounded toe of the earlier 19th century gave way to the square slightly domed toes with the square vamp.

The pair, above right, has brown leather straight slap soles that continue to the heels. They have polished finished edges and ring stamps at the toe, waist and heel. There are no back seams to the shoes and the side seams are butted. The quarters and sock are lined with white kid and the vamp with white linen with a winged heel stiffener. They are of turnshoe construction. There is a small bow at the vamp throat. One shoe has a label: 'F Marsh, maker and importer of French boots and shoes, 148 Oxford Street, opposite Bond Street' (see p. 53).

Heel: none
Size: 24cms/9½ ins

The pair, below right, has the characteristic square and slightly domed toes. The heels are of stacked painted leather with the top-piece as one with the sole. There is no back seam on the uppers but closed side seams. The quarters and insole are lined with white kid, the vamps with white linen and there is a heel stiffener. They are of turnshoe construction. The shoes are decorated with a black silk trim on the top seam and tiny black silk bows on the vamp throat. The soles are decorated with ring stamps at the toe, waist and heel. Both shoes are marked 'Mrs. Cowslade' as well as being marked 'left' and 'right'. The right shoe contains a maker's label: 'Wilson, Ladies & Gentlemen's Fashionable Boot and Shoe Maker, 19 Broad Street, Reading'.

Heel: 0.7cm/¼ in
Size: 22.9cms/9 ins

Slippers 1837-9

Black and white were traditional colours for women's boots and shoes. Cream slippers were typical evening wear whereas the black slipper tended to be formal day dress. Thin fabrics such as satin were mainly for indoor use.

The slippers shown here, and the slipper on pp. 72 and 73, are similar in style, all coming from the same maker in Norwich. The cream slipper, one of a pair, has a square toe, slightly domed, and the tan leather sole is shaped with no heel. The upper has a squared vamp throat with a draw string fastening. Extra elastic laces have been sewn in. The heel, quarters and sock are lined with white kid, and the vamp with white linen. There is a heel stiffener and it is of a turnshoe construction. The top seams are decorated with white seam binding and a white silk pleated ribbon rosette at the vamp throat.

There is a maker's label in the left shoe of the pair, 'C. Mingay, Old Established London Shoe Warehouse, No 7 Old Hay Market, Norwich'. The shoes are also marked 'Droit' and 'Gauche'. On the soles there are the numerals '37' '4' at the toes, 'M 123' at the waists and '4' on the left heel only.

Heel: none
Size: 24.8 cms/9¾ ins

The second pair is made from black silk satin. The toes are square and slightly domed and the brown leather soles are shaped right and left. The uppers have a square cut vamp throat with a V for comfort and black elastic is attached at the top seam on the quarters. The quarters and sock are lined with white kid, the vamp with white linen and there is a heel stiffener. They are of a turnshoe construction. Black silk ribbon binding decorates the top seam and there are black pleated ribbon silk rosettes on the vamps. The maker's label is in the right shoe.

Heel: none
Size: 25cms/9⅞ ins

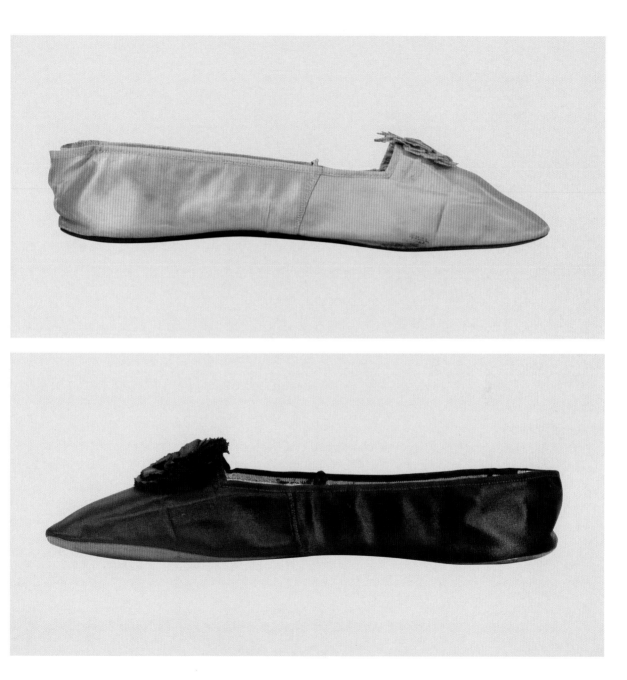

Slipper 1840s

One of a pair of cream silk satin slippers with tan leather soles shaped to right and left (see pp.88-9). The toe is square and slightly domed. The upper has a squared vamp throat. The vamp is cut in a V shape for comfort. Elastic lace is sewn in at the side seams, possibly at a later date. The shoe is darned at the inner side. The quarters and heel are lined with white kid and the vamp and sock with white linen. There is a heel stiffener. The shoe is of turnshoe construction. The top seam seams have a binding of white silk and there is a pleated white silk ribbon rosette at the vamp throat.

The maker's name appears on the left shoe: 'C Mingay, Old Established London Shoe Warehouse, No.7 Old Hay Market, Norwich'.

Heel: none
Size: 24.8cms/9¾ ins

Half Boots 1840s

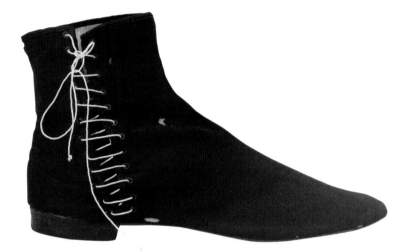

Half boots for walking or riding were fashionable throughout the 19th century. In Jane Austen's *The Watsons*, written in 1804-5, Lord Osborne tells Emma Watson 'you should wear half-boots.... Nothing sets off a neat ankle more than a half-boot.' In *Sanditon*, written by Austen shortly before her death in 1817, Mr Parker declaims 'civilisation, civilisation indeed! ....Look at William Heeley's windows. – Blue shoes and nankin Boots! – who would have expected such a sight at a Shoemaker's in old Sanditon!' Coloured boots were becoming increasingly popular.

This pair of midnight blue, fine wool half boots is typical of the period. The toe is square and shallow and the heels are stacked, painted black with a top-piece of leather. The thin soles are shaped and stop at the heel. The uppers are laced on the inside with twelve pairs of eyelets, the laces are now missing. There is an open cloth tab faced with glorious pink silk. The sides and vamps are lined with white jean (twilled cotton) and the socks with white kid. The back seams are faced with a strip of white cotton. They are of a turnshoe construction. The left and right

are marked 'H.F.Bu...(?), 71 Oxford Street', and '1437' is hand-written in the left shoe.

Heel: 1.9cms/$^3/_4$ in
Size: 26.3cms/10$^3/_8$ ins

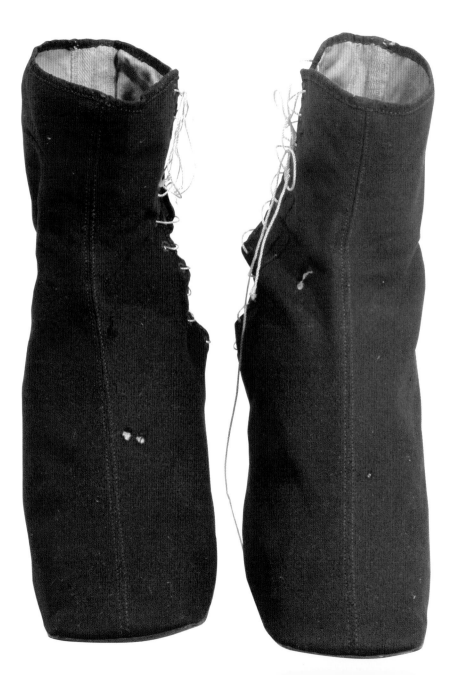

Half Boots 1840s

'A Pastoral Petticoat', an engraving from the 1840s showing a model wearing ankle boots. She is also wearing a bergère hat, recalling the shepherdess look of the previous century.

These cream kid half boots have square toes. The soles are shaped and there are no heels. There are white taped loops at the back and front of the upper and a V-shaped elastic gussets either side of the boots. The use of elastic sides was said to have been invented by J. Sparkes of Regent Street in 1837.

The linings are of cream cotton. Cream tape edged with pink decorates the back seams. They are of a turnshoe construction. The left boot has '3' written in ink at the toe. There are also remains of indistinguishable writing.

Heel: none
Size: 24.2cms/9½ ins

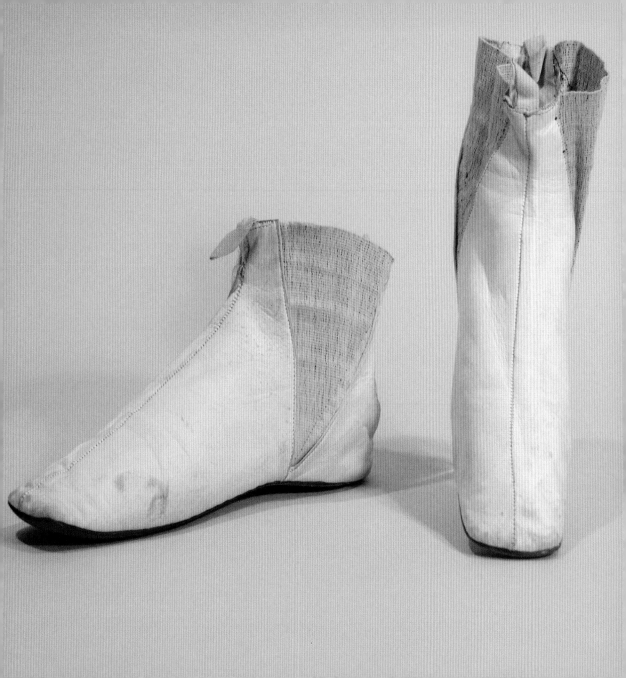

Half Boots c. 1850

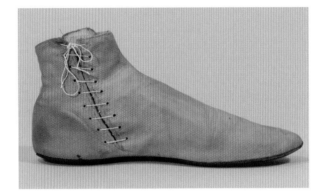

This pair of cream piqué half boots has square shallow toes with straight toe caps. The leather soles are shaped and marked '3', '2', and '1' at the waist. They have an inner side lacing with nine pairs of eyelets over an internal tongue. The laces are now missing. The quarters and vamps are lined with white linen and the insoles with stiffened white linen. There are heel stiffeners and they are of turnshoe construction.

These thin shoes and boots were soon replaced by much sturdier and more robust footwear. According to *Punch* in February 1859: 'As for thin shoes, except for dancing they appear to have vanished from the female toilet. "Balmoral" boots, soles half an inch thick, and military heels, have usurped their place. These boots and the martial red petticoats now so familiar to the eye, are to me eloquent manifestations of the change that has come over the spirit of womanhood.'

Heel: none
Size: 24.8cms/9¾ ins

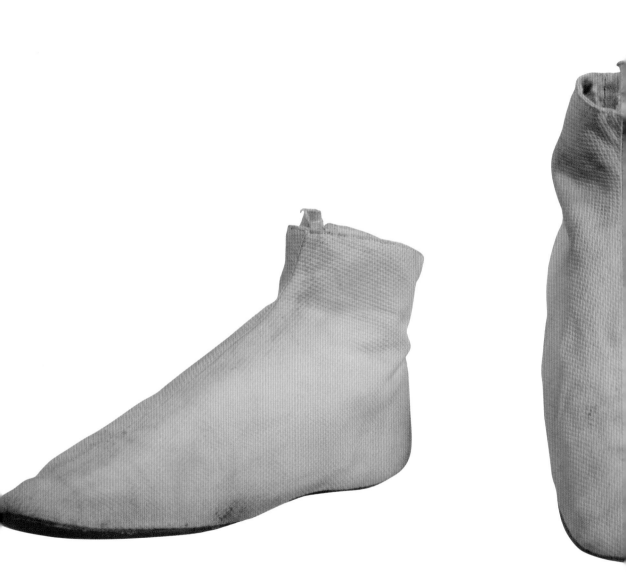

Portrait of Bruce and Caroline Chichester by J.E. Williams, painted in 1849 and now at Arlington Court in Devon. Both children are shown in Arab dress, including exotic slippers.

These slippers are widely dated to the first half of the 19th century, and may well have been imported from Turkey or the Middle East. They are made from red leather and have square, slightly domed toes and no heel. The brown leather slap soles are shaped and decorated with three ring stamps. The vamps extend to small tongues which may have previously been loops for a lace but have been cut away. The slippers were fastened by laces at the vamp, throat, instep and back. The lining of white cotton is sewn to the welt and there is a white cotton sock. They are of turnshoe construction. Red silk decorates the top band.

Heel: none
Size: 26.4cms/$10^3/_8$ ins

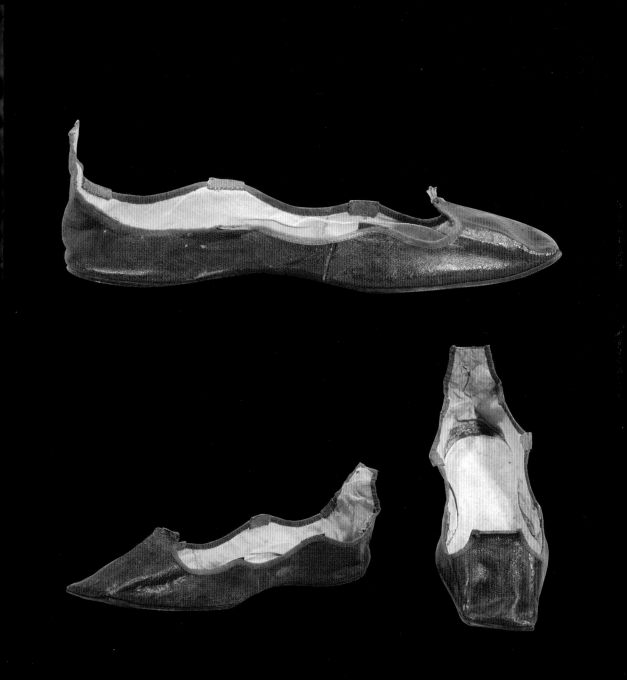

Slippers c. 1850

This pattern for Berlin woolwork would have been supplied with the coloured yarns as a guide for amateur embroiderers.

Needlework, known as Berlin woolwork, became a very popular pastime for ladies of leisure during the Victorian period. The brighter colours available with the invention of aniline dyes brought a greater vibrancy to fashion.

This pair of slippers is made from cream, brown, black and beryl blue Berlin wool on canvas in a diamond lattice with graded infill. The toes are square and the left and right soles are slightly shaped (see pp. 88-9). The vamp throat is square cut. The beryl blue silk linings are quilted on the sock and there are white kid heel grips. They are of turnshoe construction. Beryl blue ribbon decorates the top seams and the tan leather sole is marked at the toe, waist, and heel with three ringed punch marks.

Heel: none
Size: 23.5cms/9¼ ins

Shoes 1850s

In the mid-Victorian period, shoes gradually began to re-adopt heels. The *Ladies Cabinet* for 1850 comments: 'somewhat high-heeled shoes are becoming general, not only for walking, but for the ballroom'. These are generally shaped and quite stocky, a few centimetres or an inch or so in height.

This pair of shoes has cream silk uppers and heel coverings. The toes are square and slightly domed and the heels covered and shaped with top-pieces of leather. The brown leather soles are straights. The vamps have a square throat and there are drawstrings. The shoes show evidence of repair at the heel and side seams. The quarters are lined with black kid, the sides with cotton, and they have a white kid sock. There is yellow stitching on the insoles. The shoes are of turnshoe construction. The shoes are decorated with maroon bows with fringed edges and central vertical strips at the vamp throats. A stamp on the soles reads ' MAYER A PARIS ' with '(?) Julien' written in the middle. There is also a crown above the stamp and '27' below the stamp on one shoe only.

Heel : 4.5cms/1⅜ ins
Size: 24.3cms/9½ ins

Shoes Second half of 19th century

English fashion plate for April 1864. The model in the foreground is wearing low-heeled black shoes with rosettes under her crinoline.

Empress Eugénie, the very stylish consort of Napoleon III of France, encouraged a trend in the 1860s for stockings to match the dress. Up to this time, the colour of stockings generally complemented rather than matched that of shoes.

These fine black silk shoes have shaped and covered heels with top-pieces of leather attached with brass nails. The toes are rounded, up-turned and slightly curved. The leather soles are shaped left and right. The quarters and socks are lined with black leather and the vamp with black linen. The heels have a stiffener. They are of turnshoe construction with a welt. The vamps are decorated with beaded flower type rosettes. Ribbon bows have been inserted at a later date.

Heel: 2.8cms/1¹/₈ ins
Size: 23.5cms/9¹/₄ ins

Shoe-making

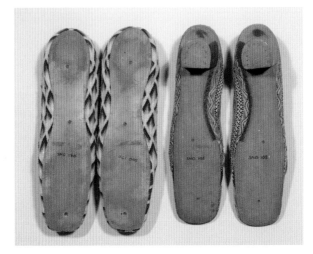

Until the mid-19th century, shoes had identical, straight soles and the same uppers. This was a style that stemmed from practicality, although it was exploited by fashion at various periods. The pair of shoes on the left, dating from the 1850s, have almost identical soles, taking on the shape of left and right through wear alone, although the shoe-maker might mark each shoe for left or right use. As the century progressed, the increase in mechanisation and demand led to more styled footwear with the left and right shoes clearly distinguished. This can be seen in the pair of shoes, dating from the 1870s, on the right-hand side of the picture.

The cobbler's bench on display at Snowshill Manor reflects the observations made by Charles Wade in his notebooks about the small Suffolk village of Yoxford, where he grew up. Like so many villages at the end of the 19th century, Yoxford could support numerous local craftsmen and a shop that provided anything from groceries to draperies and hardware. Wade recalled 'Ezra', the carpenter 'who inherited none of the skills of his forefathers' and who always wrought considerable damage when doing a repair. Of the cobbler, Sam Thurlow, Wade wrote, 'a little man with a little shop and a little bench

containing all his tools. To his lasts were sprigged pieces of leather moulded to the corns and bunions of his customers' feet. The lasts had his customers' names inscribed upon them. So, round the walls of the shop was recorded some intimate village history.'

Shoes 1870

These shoes, whilst having a similar profile to those on pp. 86 and 87, are distinguished by their brass-covered shaped heels (see frontispiece). The uppers are made from cream, black, green, red and blue woven wool and silk. The toes are square and shallow. The brown leather soles are shaped. The uppers have square vamps and vamp throats and a drawstring at the top band. The lining is of green silk with a green sock with red silk binding. There is white stitching at the instep and heel stiffeners. They are of a turnshoe construction. The top band is decorated with red silk with white stitching and there are rosettes of pink silk with gilt buttons at their centres on the vamps. On the sole there are pinpoint stamps at the tread and instep and a red leather instep band with pinpoint zigzag decoration. There is a maker's leather label at the instep, '(?) Virga Calzolaio' indicating probable Italian manufacture.

Heel: 3.8cms/1 ½ ins
Size: 24cms/9 ¼ ins

The latest Paris dresses from The Queen, *October 1884, showing how high-heeled shoes were worn with the bustles that were the fashion of the period.*

As the century progressed the square toe developed from the rounded profile to a blunt point in the late 1870s. This pair of satin shoes has covered heels and blunt toes. The shaped and covered heels have top-pieces of leather and six brass studs. The leather soles are shaped and end at the base of the heel breast. The quarters, heels and socks have a black leather lining, the vamp black linen, and there are heel stiffeners. At some time there have been black ties of elastic from the top of the side seams. The shoes are decorated with black silk bows.

Heel: 5cms/2 ins
Size: 24.3cms/9½ ins

Glossary

BACK STRAP a strip of material covering the back seam

HEEL composed of the BREAST (the front of the heel under the arch), the TOP-PIECE (the part of the heel that comes into contact with the ground, called the top because during manufacture the shoe is worked upside down) and the SEAT (the concave part of the heel that fits to the shoe and which houses the foot)

INSOLE a piece of leather or other material between the sole and the foot

LAST generally made from wood, on which the shoe is made. The shape resembles the desired shoe, and is often hinged to allow for ease of removal once the shoe is formed

LATCHETS the top of the uppers that extend from the quarters, crossing over at the front of the shoe

QUARTER the back of the shoe which meets the vamp, so-called because it is in effect a quarter of the shoe

RAND a narrow strip of leather in the sole or heel seams

SOCK material inside the shoe covering all or part of the insole, but not to be confused with the insole

SOLE STAMP sealed holes made by nails, used to attach the soles to the last before attaching the upper

STIFFENER the reinforcement of the quarters, usually giving extra support to the back

THROAT the front of the vamp

TONGUE an extension of the vamp under the latchets

TURNSHOE a method of constructing the shoe where it is made inside out before being turned so that the sole seam is on the inside

UPPERS the part of the shoe that covers the top of the foot, normally consisting of the vamp, quarters and lining

VAMP the front section of the upper covering the toes and part of the instep

WAIST the part of the shoe that corresponds to the instep and the arch of the foot

WELT a narrow strip of leather sewn round the edge of the upper and insole prior to the attachment of the sole to both

WHEELING decoration with an iron wheeled over the sole and seat seams to seal them producing ridged or fancy patterns

Shoe Diagram

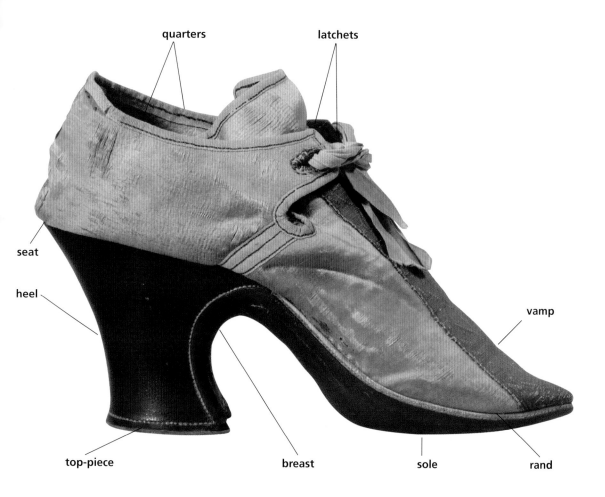

quarters

latchets

seat

heel

vamp

top-piece

breast

sole

rand

First published in Great Britain in 2004
by National Trust Enterprises Limited,
36 Queen Anne's Gate, London SW1H 9AS

www.nationaltrust.org.uk

ISBN 0 7078 0385 3   391.413   MCK

Designed by SMITH
Editorial and picture research by Margaret Willes
Colour origination by Digital Imaging Ltd. Glasgow
Printed in China by WKT Co. Ltd.

Picture Credits
The Wade Collection pictures were photographed by Richard
Blakey. Other illustrations: NTPL/John Hammond, pp.6.8;
NTPL/Andreas von Einsiedel, pp.10,12; Lord Feversham,
Duncombe Park, p.20; NT/Cameracraft, p.24; NTPL/Andreas von
Einsiedel, pp.30,36; NTPL/Roy Fox, p.38; Hereford Museum,
p.50; NTPL/Roy Fox, p.53; NTPL/John Hammond, p.58;
Hereford Museum, pp.68,76; NTPL/John Hammond, p.80;
Hereford Museum, p.86; NTPL/Andreas von Einsiedel, p.89;
Hereford Museum, p.92.

Cover: Brocade shoes, 1740s (see pp. 22 and 23)
Half-title: Slippers, 1810-30 (see pp. 50 and 51)
Frontispiece: Heel of shoe, 1870s (see pp. 90 and 91)
Title: Satin shoe, 1740s (see pp. 22 and 23)